WHAT LOVE TELLS ME

What Love Tells Me

Richard Waring

Richard Waring

Poems

For Ed & Linda,
spirited good
friends.
Belmont, 12/4/16

Word Poetry

Published by Word Poetry
P.O. Box 541106
Cincinnati, OH 45254-1106

ISBN: 978-1-62549-202-9

Poetry Editor: Kevin Walzer
Business Editor: Lori Jareo

Visit us on the web at www.wordpoetrybooks.com

Cover photo: *Tree and Stone*, Jordan Pond Trail, Mount Desert Island, Maine, by the author

What the Flowers Tell Me
What the Animals Tell Me
What the Angels Tell Me
What Love Tells Me

— working titles for sections of Mahler's Third Symphony

Acknowledgments

I am grateful to the following publications and their editors, where portions of this work, sometimes in different form, first appeared:

The American Journal of Nursing: "Oboe"
Chest: "I Give My Brother a Kidney"
The Comstock Review: "The Museum of Me" and "At the Skate Park"
Inward Springs: "Aftermath"
JAMA, Journal of the American Medical Association: "Gurney"
Sanctuary, Journal of the Massachusetts Audubon Society:
    "In Tall Grass" and "Luxury Townhouses"

"In Tall Grass" was installed on a stone pillar in Edmands Park, Newton, MA, as part of its Poetry in the Park Project.

Special thanks to Barbara Helfgott Hyett, mentor and unconditional friend, Grey Held and Robin Pelzman, initial readers and commentators, Wendy Drexler for invaluable suggestions, and the dedicated members of the Workshop for Publishing Poets (www.poemworks.com). To Star Island, my spirit's home, and the Conference on the Arts (www.stararts.org), where I received inspiration from Nancy Willard, Simone Muench, Jack McCarthy, Ellen Schmidt, Barbara Kasselmann, Poppy Brandes, Nicole Terez Dutton, and Regie Gibson, among many others. To my mother, father, and brothers for their long-sustaining love. Most of all, to my soul's mate, my wife, for her incomparable spirit and wisdom.

for my children,
Cornelia and Sam

Contents

III.

I.

Birth

My wife closes her eyes
        to the fierce light,
                her animal strength spent,
      while I study the several chins
of our daughter — blue and otherworldly —
                her shoulders so broad I wonder
      what I can say to ally
the anguish of that passage.

Until she cries.

Her eyes widen as she sees
        the two of us who have
                made her up. Her head
        smells like the earth after rain
before the nurse takes her to
                intensive care and my wife
        hemorrhages and nearly bleeds out.
They staunch and sew, replenish.

Then we are alone with our hands,
        the blind hunger of our hands.

Acute Care Pediatric Ward

She lies waiting in an isolette
  like Moses ready to be carried
    downstream. A nurse sluices medicine
      through tubes into her scalp.

I've come with her mother's milk,
  that precious cargo I've learned
    to navigate Storrow Drive
      to bring to the hospital.

I am her fulcrum-father, holding
  my week-old daughter who lifts
    the bottle to her lips
      like a supple diety.

When she turns away, suck-sated,
  I tell the story of our joy
    at her becoming, the shoring
      of our lives still days away,
        this clean connection
          all we've ever known.

Doll

My daughter brought her home,
a foundling from the dust heap
      of a forgotten street.

Nothing I'd ever bought her
could compare. New things are easy
      to love, joy coming right from the wrapper.

This had an unclothed, filthy provenance,
one eye glued shut as if dreaming,
      one eye missing

      its lashes, starkly staring,
the kind of doll not just anyone can love.
You have to be called.

Bowling with My Son

He pushes each ball off on its spinning axis
   down the oiled alley, past the wobbly
      pull of gutters, to bang the pins
         left standing into new configurations.

This calms his fear that the button
   on his nightshirt is the eye of a dog,
      that he was once a god, that his head
         is too small for his vocabulary.

I believe in the trinity of holes, soothed
   by how more pins glide magically down
      for the next round like a host
         of new angels sent to save us.

Yellow Jackets

They come out of hiding —
 from nowhere.
  Quick fire spreads
   to the four corners
    of my daughter's tiny frame.

This is the grim recital of how
 small things come weighted
  and how her throat —
   that avenue to all else —
    can close.

In Tall Grass

Over and over, the grasses part
    for winds that will never give up
        swelling, cresting, receding back
            on themselves, wrapping around us.

We are glittering like the metallic green
    of a tiger beetle, unhinged for flight,
        alive in a field where so much
            awaits, the mossy sorrows,

the grasshopping surprises. We fall
    in love with all that is not
        ours, this particular firefly,
            that determined stalk of yarrow.

Leaving the woods is a sadness,
    returning home a vague diminishment,
        that we are father and son and not
            some wild things in the night.

At the Skate Park

Head shaved, chest bare, poise
   in a hurry, my son powers up
      for a heelflip backside one-eighty out.
   Bearings ram to tarmac
with a switch hardflip. He gets
   his claw on the nose
      and does a magic snatch-up
   to a crooked grind, battling
down a double-barreled park rail.

I am with him on each bump and ollie,
   catching frontside air, then summoning
      gravity as a new friend. I want
   to quit my job, work that hard
to groom the moves of a dancer.
   He's ready to create some swooping
      scoop action leading to a fifty-fifty stall,
   as if split shins were only virtual,
when he suddenly wings himself away.

Marriage

When we speak, our words
    are freighted as a cargo ship,
        tarantulas hidden among the bananas.

Sometimes I swallow
    spiders in my sleep.
        I don't sleep well these nights.

Tree

No, she says, *it's over.*

We're driving south
   on a scarified highway
      after bringing our son to camp.

My childhood inspiration —
   a beech tree that had been around
      since George Washington — was so
         unyielding they had to build
            the street on either side.

I want to be that tree, that road,
   something that endures.
      She blinks away the few
         tears that surface, hands love back
         to me, plump as blackberries
            by the side of a dirt road.

Shattered

My son flings
    the wedding portrait
        against a wall, tosses
            the wine glass he always said
            looks like the Holy Grail
                into the fireplace, takes
                    an ax to his treehouse.

Weeks go by without
    a word. He is suffering
        the way a Jack pine suffers,
            tight cones opening
            only after fire.

I snap, slap his
    face. His mouth
        turns down, his
            eyes radiate rage.
                I am the father
                    I swore I'd never be.

Gurney

The policeman descends
the innocent stairs
with my son behind him,
through the house of sharp objects
into the shame of day.

At the back of the ambulance
the cop says, *Lie down,* but my son won't
and I have to lift him onto the gurney,
into the restraints, his weight
heavy as betrayal.

He works free.
The EMT says, *Are you going
to cooperate or not?*
The boy I love lifts his head,
shouts, *I hate you all.*

There are many words
for heartbreak, and none.
He lets his head sink down
and they take him.

Oboe

When he is alone in the locked ward
   of the children's unit, he picks up
      his oboe to hold off the screams,
         the heads banging the wall.

His hands grasp Mozart and Bach,
   the grammar of a new survival.
      The nurses put their clipboards
         down to listen.

The Beatles are singing in the cafeteria:
   There's nothing you can do
      that can't be done. I want to believe
         all you need is love, the way the nurses

believe in his music as he gathers up
   the silence, every valve open
      in his heart, that first instrument,
         the one that tunes all the rest.

Watching My Son Make a Reed

You take the cane that comes
all the way from southern France,
hollow it on your gouging machine,
place it on the shaper tip,
and run a razor down.

You carve your heart out
along its windows, rub the back
to thinnest vanishing, reveal
your eliding spine, coax tones
that are like nothing in this world.

I never taught you to shave
yet you hone your life on a stone,
shape with ease, applying beeswax
to your thread, counting
the wraparounds and tying off.

You toil in silence for something
beyond sunlight, moisture, tongue, breath,
fingers moving to improve what nature
gave you, wrestling perfection
into a note's first song.

Every sorrow leads to this: a longing
happy enough to climb a scale.
This is how you know what will be
your cry. The crow trembles.
The reed slides gently into place.

Recital

He is pure
amid a frenzy
of strings and
bows, the dark
wood of his song
hard as stone. Once
he played with emptiness.
Now he moves the wind
to summon amazement.
Sounding a clarion A, he holds
to every note, its height, its depth,
bar by bar, his bridge, his will, his way out.

Hummingbird

I find him
        lying on the sidewalk,
    sink to my knees,
lift that breath,
    the needle beak, tongue
        as thin as thread, feathers
    translucent, already
beginning to disappear.

I keep him all night in a basket
        on my kitchen table
    as I coax
sugar water from a thimble.
    I have never taken in anything
        so beautiful. Every night
    for a week I hoped
he would live

long enough
        for the patch of ruby
    to flush along his throat,
for wings to beat to blurred haste
    and vanish over the roof.

She Takes Her Wedding Band Off

and there they all are,
 every girlfriend I ever had,
  as if I'd rubbed some lamp.

There's the one with the *open*
 sesame kiss who gave me
  my first hickey. I wore a lot
   of turtlenecks that year.

There's the one I lost
 my virginity to who later
  tried her hand at suicide.

And look — it's the thrifty one,
 insisting we reuse condoms
  after washing and drying them
   with corn starch and hot breath.

None of them has aged.
 All of them want me.
  I take my ring off, too.

When I Loved Her

Food was just a prop
we pushed around
like giants herding sheep.

We fed on the self
and self-admiring.

I believed in permanence,
sunstruck rocks
that never grow cold.

Each kiss bordered
on belief.

Now I feast on the best cuts,
medallions and chops
from the slaughterhouse lamb.

Settlement

How can I separate
    my belongings from hers?

The soup tureen
from her Aunt Susie
      matches my china.

      The chrome
toaster, a birthday present,
is mine, but the kitchen
table that was mine
I give to her.

      The hedge clippers
she wields the day I leave,
a gift from my parents,
she can also have.

I won't need them
where I'm going. We trade
      portraits of our children
like pieces of gold.

Finally, she gives me
    the bed. *Too much
history,* she says.

Winter

Leaves
form the pages
of winter's diary.

The crook
of a maple
reveals a bruise

of yellow
feathers, the wing
of a moth.

Year Apart

I stop shaving, begin
no new hobbies.
Have to get a room
with a friend, everything
awkward again. It's
The Year of Not Doing
Anything Stupid.

I take his books on divorce
off the shelf and read them.
He hasn't, so I fill him in.
We drink wine at lunch
and listen to what
Miles Davis has to say.

Summer becomes fall.
He mows barefoot. I don't.
He goes another season not taking
the Parents Without Partners class.
I do and learn that people aren't
there to make you happy,
they're there to make you grow.

I grow.

Between

My son gets out of the family
car, enters the realm between
my care and his mother's. Suffering
is the fastest mode of transportation.

He treads the thin walkway
that balances what's tried and true
with what is not yet found, every crack
a precarious place to stand.

When will I see him again? I worry
the distance, knowing each step offers
fresh reason for hope or delay.

We sleep in separate homes,
close enough to count the same
sheep, our lunate bodies turning
different ways in the nameless hour.

Hansel and Gretel

Their father forced them
far from their world. Sparrows flew off,
left them alone with their hands.
Stones could not say
where they had been.

Come in, said the old woman, opening
the oven door just for the hell of it.
She taught Gretel to stop looking
over her shoulder, put Hansel in a cage.
Wouldn't we be better off, she said, *without boys?*

Those children roamed a chastity of stars,
hiding sorrow like a bad tooth.
Morning sun warmed without succor.
Aimless as trees, everywhere a dare,
they came home.

Moth

The caterpillar emerges
    from a white seed
        the size of a sesame.

Fattened on birch leaves,
    it splits into orange, grows bold,
        splits again into succulent green,
            tufts of quills down both sides.

Three instars.

It is ready to draw silk, vanish
    into a realm as dark as Houdini's,
        melt and rearrange, wings
          weaving thin air into
            moons and eyespots.

It makes passage through
    a secret slit, dries on bark,
        resolves into night.

Divorce

The children are still
ours, even as husband and wife
fall away. We circle them
in singular orbits.

They go about their lives
in the aftermath, this boy,
this girl, factor time
into calculations.

The sun braids bands of gold
in their mother's brown eyes,
though she looks
elsewhere.

Trees reach up, bees breeze by,
and a walk down the street
is still a walk down the street.
What are we to each other?

The power to cherish
or ruin, to find what stones
of happiness might last.
To call that enough.

Putting Down the Family Dog

Once we searched for hours, desperate
to claim him before coyotes did,
refusing to go home until he was found.

Now we are here, unspoused,
our broken-backed dog between us,
as the vet injects the shot.

His eyes brighten, subside —
our historian of smell, our silent
witness — another link lost.

Night

Breath is something I share
with the bruised grays of evening.
I watch as light calls itself home,
descending a flight of stairs and leaving
the shadows to play among themselves.

Slowly, as I listen, sky
is a new liquidity. *Drink me.*
I am the keeper of lost knucklebones.
I will make sorrow seem sweet.

Not to be outdone, the moon shows up,
goes traipsing until it meets the distant
city, plunges beneath the kindred kindling
of neon and I speak at last
with Orion and his dogs.

Monarchs Passing Through New England

They arrive in September,
storm kings, landing in lilacs,
chitinous orange frames
leaf-heavy, a new kind of foliage.

Scientists say they make
a right-hand turn in the middle
of Lake Superior, a blind thirst
to follow an ancient, long-gone glacier.

They turn singularity
into collective, a wave of wings
craving an updraft, a rise over the Empire
State Building like any mountain,

spreading the arms of summer
across a continent. I, too, ache to make
a wild dogleg turn, to rise and fall,
fit tongue and groove into a new story.

II.

My Older Brother

We play in front of the fireplace,
my older brother thin as Laurel,
and I, heavy as Hardy.

Our mother's face is as hopeful
as the pin-ups in my father's World
War II deck of cards.

Father has jet black hair,
not yet combed over.

This is before diabetes
resets our clocks. I have one
untried heart, two kidneys.

Nothing has yet been asked for.
Nothing has yet been given.
We are the family before anything happens.

In the Church Pew

My mother knows
all the words, doubts
nothing, her eyes serene,
hazel commingling with the spot of brown.

Her hands are married to the prayer
for my brother's disease. Her diamond
ring glints like facets of our Lord.
Her knees rest on the cushions
of that love.

Bee

Because he's allergic
and I hate him right now,
I foist a bee on my finger
in front of my brother's face
right at the family cookout.

I know he will shoot
into the house while the roses
brim with beauty and mother
changes his dressing of tears.

I am a child who seems
to speak only the language of petals,
their many tongues carrying
messages on the wind.

Clouds go by with their
sleights-of-hand, their scarves
that open like thresholds of night
outside our home on the hill.

Wondering About My Younger Brother

When he was a boy, did he sense
    that we were lost, that we ached
        for him to join in the faintest starlight?

If he gave up his shadow
    I would have suffered, too,
        unhooked from his shade.

Who would have burned brighter then?

Goldilocks

grew restless
at the idea of no return,
no change of attitude.

She knocked
and the bears could barely
contain their joy.

Come in! Sit down! they said,
marveling at her even temper,
her mannered way.

The young cub, no longer
spoiled, took one good look
and thought, just right.

My Remington

This is the writing machine of my grandfather's
blindness as he felt for the centering dots of *F* and *J*.
This is the writing machine of my father's
two-fingered *click clack-clack* branding
the stippled page with his thoughts.

This is my regal Remington, its hinged
platform and the steep incline of its keys —
like elaborate holders for tiddlywinks —
tiny terraces casting their *QWERTY*
eyes on me, the solitary rememberer.

My fingers move like planchettes on casters.
O many-layered oracle that sweeps
the return of the roller. O holder of my poems,
the ribboned dawning of each new line.
And at the end, the small wonder of the bell!

The Summer I Made Hard Hats

I worked the night shift, pushed buttons
to close the injection molding machine,
squeezing plastic through a narrow gate.
Reaching in, I'd pull the helmet from its womb,
snip the flashing, lay it under the drill bit,
plunge and carve the nub smooth.

Sometimes I got bored
and threw a piece of flashing
into the works to grind the machine
to a halt. Then the handicapped
men and women on the assembly line
would not be able to glue
comfort pads or attach chin straps
for which they got paid by the piece.

It was the summer I read Eliot
and made up the tune for
The Love Song of J. Alfred Prufrock.
Above the hum of gears I'd sing
In the room, the women come and go
talking of Michaelangelo, Michaelangelo,
knowing I'd be back in school after this stint,
knowing I hadn't lived enough, learned enough
to be ashamed.

Sleeping with Allen Ginsberg

I loll on the bunk
as he plays his harmonium
and explains how this
is the very spot
where Blake spoke to him,
gave him permission, anointed him
with the whispered transmission.

He puts down the squeezebox,
lies beside me, reverently bends
to take me into himself and I plunge
as Allen had plunged into Neal Cassidy
and Neal plunged into Gavin
and Gavin into Ed
and Ed into Walt Whitman
and Walt had plunged
into America.

Next morning, I wander
in the bearded light,
Blake's gravelly voice licking my ear,
the teapot full-throated in the kitchen,
Peter Orlovsky yodeling ecstatic in the spare bedroom,
books in their floor-to-ceiling splendor.
Everything open.

Jack and Jill

Why did they go
in the first place?

Couldn't whoever
filled the pail fetch it?

If her name was Mary
they'd be on the prairie.

Jill, tumbling after,
didn't even break a nail.

Only later did Jack become
nimble and quick, a jack

of all trades. That house
he built had solid plumbing.

The pail was relegated
to the barn. Jill, after that

one amazing routine,
was never heard from again.

Luxury Townhouses

The boys who'd loved these trails
got swallowed by jobs.

They left the owls and salamanders
to move about on their own.

Our woods became anybody's.
Nobody's. Sitting in our cubicles,

we saw trees fall like toothpicks,
got used to dynamite the way

fish get used to waterfalls. One day,
during lunch break, we watched

a deer venture out of the woods
onto the light-struck hill

then vanish
back into what was left.

Song of Origin

I enumerate my meandering existence,
    revel in revealing the nuanced places,
        wander past banks and dreams and trees.

Show me the place where sky cries,
    the distance between what flowers tell me
        and what love tells me, the joyously

grieving way things are. Cover me
    with hints until I'm let out into a lake.
        I'll go down in the hollows and come up

for air just to flick my clouds away
    until the mountains appear below
        as clear as a problem resolved.

My tongue will grow restless, ache for the next
    plunge through rain-drenched rapids,
        for all the necessary and rough news.

I Give My Brother a Kidney

After our well-wishers leave the hospital,
he comes to my room in his face mask
full of gratitude, my big brother,
and we talk as we haven't
among the tubes of our bedside existence.

They left us once, our parents,
and he put on the classical record
from the red boxed set. We danced
around the turntable in our footed sleepers,
making the room dizzy, and left

this world to spin through carpetless
space, bits of destiny, joy into joy,
like the vision I had, under my eyelids,
waking out of surgery to the two lights
merging, our arms holding everything there is.

Scar

I look in the mirror, run
a finger up and down the sleek
sigmoid curve that sweeps
like a riverbed beneath my ribs.

I've lived years, unscarred,
two perfect kidneys turning
the cells of my marrow
pink as a rose.

This gift, so the cells
of my brother's marrow
with turn pink, too, this
alchemy without boundaries,

this one kidney, which is
beginning to belong
to him, newly taken,
no longer mine.

Climbing the Maple

In the still moss of evening
I take whatever comes
into my arms. I am cultivating
courage one branch at a time,
listening for the story only bark
can tell, my brothers in the rings.

I am on high, my bed
of tallest wood alive
to my touch, ascending limb
by glamorous limb into
the whisperings of all
I've wanted to know.

By morning I wake in the white
somewhere. From here I can
smell the uncut loam and heaven's
breath. Voices judge me strong,
wash my eyes until nothing
can be taken from their radiance.

Ants bury their dead, beetles
carry last words into the ground.
In the tree top, I learn
and unlearn the language
of wind — every twig unbowed,
each tip, newly minted.

III.

Out of the Blue

We were lying on your living
room floor and reading
how to French kiss when you
told me I could put my hand
on your tank top, which happened
to be where your breasts were,
which was the point, you said.
We tried that kiss and the tea
kettle blew, before anyone
knew about us and our longing,
before you took up with the baker
and I married someone else, before
I divorced someone else and you
called from the Baja out of the blue
to say that the reason we'd broken
up was that you were afraid
to have sex and that you
weren't afraid anymore.

After Divorce

I thought of becoming
a monk, not in an organized way
but as a consequence, hiding
behind a stupifying beard.

Instead, I took a lover
who prepared me for fire
after years of a flickering marriage
with no more wood.

I wept in the ravenous light,
tasting a little of what I'd missed,
the hurt moving out

of my bones with a glacier's oblivion,
my mind alive to a sudden
tongue-tied freedom.

Peninsula

Because I'd been
  hollowed out
    by sorrow
  for so long,
the Baja had
  everything
  I wanted:
    wine and olives,
      the improvisations
of salt, figs, goat
    cheese. I ate
      to certify
    my life among
  century-old cacti,
  once more at play,
stepping out from
  the palapas to
      pelicans lifting
        magnificent,
          slowly flapping
          wings.

Mexico

Lizards sun themselves.
In the room, your body
burns like an oleander.

Your eyes are the blue
Sea of Cortez. Deep in the swell,
the moon slips past.

Let me kiss your breasts!
Salt of your lips
brings me through.

Kiss

Night lies in the rough
sky of your palate, molten,
mouthed into creation.

Lips press against infinity,
tongues need no words,
ladders to the moon.

In the longing for flight,
we are the domed halves
of happiness

in witness
to this breath, this bliss,
no matter the wreckage.

Pelicans

Their foreheads praise
the air sacs in their skin
when they dive into water
sixty feet down.

Their wings flap
slower than any other bird.
Their bills are ten-gallon hats.
Let the loaves and fishes jump in!

They've got cloacas
like you've never seen,
love muscles on mescaline,
aerial bayonets, rampant rammers.

They don't crow about this.
They have no song.
Certain Indians worship them
as gods, and rightly so.

Diving at Cabo San Luca

> *I am made whole by my scars.*
> —Samuel Menashe

Newly gilled, my arms
outstretched, a crazy poetfish.
Wrasses and barbers and wounds.

The brisk business of discovery
makes me swoon. Sea stars
are patterned like an alternate sky!

I swim among creatures I have yet
to name, dipped in purple,
edged with neon.

A school of barracuda
shows up, all teeth
and silver shards.

I have not dallied
with beauty
long enough.

Lover

Undress every corner
from floorboards to rafters. Nourish
the imagination of your palms.

Open buttons with the delicacy
of a love letter sealed with wax.
The body is a country of happiness.

Every view is solace.
Give flight like a tiger swallowtail
that has never known winter.

There will be time for the body
politic, for the salamander slipping
out of fire into its vernal pool.

Hold hope in your arms for pleasure.
Stretch yourself, moist clay
between here and the sky.

Brim and rebrim
every petal of being.
Love this, love this.

Last Night and Today

Last night I poured tears from my eyes.
    One eye flowed sadness, the other joy,
        and my mouth introduced them
            as long-lost cousins.

I cupped a hand under each weeping eye
    to find out which was heavier,
        to see if there was something
            I might learn from love.

Today mist rises and shrugs off the mountains
    and their nighttime wanderings.
        A warbler in the tree top
            knows this and sings.

Spoon

I'm placed on the table
the night before, hold
moonlight no one else sees.

Mornings: stirring,
scooping, being licked.
Someone drums me.

On the serving platter,
I orbit a circle of hands before
the orgy of the dishwasher.

The touch of towel is better
than the slow tongue of air.
When it's time to sink

back into chastity, I relish
the company of tines and knives,
their serated anonymity.

Fortune Cookie

Now is the time.
Let your ambition take you.

Anger and jealousy should not
succeed beyond expectation.

Make the one ahead of you
become lax in worldly ways.

You will win a high prize
or fall out of an airplane.

Try to be exuberant.
The whole world believes.

Happiness

for Eric Hyett

Completely implausible, unsustainable,
fickle as a button on an heirloom sweater.
My face needs to be remade.

Happiness is a god, being everywhere and nowhere,
an astronaut returning to earth
with fresh news.

Its impermanence is a monument, a mountain's
dark sidekick, a river slipping casually
toward some ocean.

Of course it can't last, it only seems
boundless, unlimited,
an endangered species of once.

Aftermath

Stay clear of the abyss,
with its sadness and indifference.
No oasis from the dust inside your heart.
The shoes and wallets will be
gathered. Many will go unsung.
Be as Liberty, still greening
against a backdrop of gray despair.

Whatever is down there,
once a part of the irreducible machinery,
is now a shimmering disassembling
that valorizes, vaporizes human feeling
as it sighs, dies, cascades back to bedrock.

Rising in the morning, I go
to my window, look out
at my city and what's missing,
those two front teeth and the pits
I've been endlessly worrying over.
I listen to the exquisite throbbing
of my heart that lives, in spite of everything,
in the radiant lap of today.

Scat

I enter the woods
   along a river trail, turn
      down the nearest deer path.
As the way grows faint,
   I wake.

Here a leopard frog
   spends life unwatched.
      A row of mushrooms marks
the grave where a maple fell.
   Scat shows traces of hair,
      of dreamberries.

A flash of tail has me scurrying
   to see more, to glimpse
      a being in this world
I don't yet know. Seeing her
   may make all the difference
      between living and something better.

World without Fear

Optimism hangs around
    like my younger brother, ready
        with dark coffee and conversation.

I am as frisky as the earth
    over a child's cat's grave. Even
        the mailman is a welcome sight.

My poems have become strong
    as the aroma of a Spanish guitar.
        Life takes on the shape

of a hat that a neighbor wears
    who grows plums in her garden.
        If you want me,

come around back. I'll be tossing
    my sorrow in a pit,
        covering it with loam.

How It Works

I wonder at their intentions,
    these poems that tell of life
        beyond my own, now and then
            delivering a blowdart to the head.

Sometimes the words are a balm
    spun right from the tongue, sometimes
        a haunting glimpse of something seminal,
            coalescing in a deep recess.

Whether the mind leeches poison
    or perfume, my hand must claim
        the solitary evidence, cooling coals
            by the heat of a tutelary music,

before words recede back into their thickets
    and furrows, before night tightens the lids
        of the encampment and the poem
            clears out.

The Museum of Me

Welcome to the Museum of Me.
In this first room is a collection
of insects, the brethren of my childhood:
the yard-marching stag beetle, busy
as a businessman, an ant wielding
a wheat flake, a monarch freed from
its gold-banded chrysalis.

                    Next
is a corridor of trees: the elm
behind which I savored my first kiss,
the giant maple, its boughs inviting
ascent, the beech tree, a secret etching place
for the heart. The exhibit is best viewed
from forty feet up.

                    Climb to the next
exhibit: one tree to a room without regrets.
It promotes daydreams. Another leads to a domain
of discards, one for each year: the Smurf
with orange hair, a collection of 45s, the jockstrap
with its triumphant cup.

                    Eventually you'll come
to a hall of mirrors: the one I looked into
as zits grew, the one that held my first shave.
In another I practiced kissing and marveled
at the magic of moving hands. I saw
what no one else saw and what everyone
already knew.

Pass through this hall
to the main gallery, where mentors and lovers
are remembered, some for a single phrase,
others for bringing about a whole new era.
Over here is the man who delivered me
from shyness, and there's the girl who stroked
my hair at a dance.

The last room is still
in progress. My children guard the details.
I have no idea what you'll find. I go, sometimes,
to gather my thoughts. You can picnic in the grass
if you want. Stay as long as you like.

Things I Have Learned

Fear appears daily,
like a beard, and daily
I shave it off.

Whenever it rains,
I am lonely
for the clouds.

I like my saviors
firmly standing,
not nailed up high.

Earth has yet to be
praised enough.
Lilacs, for instance.

People are fantastic.
People are the only
inhibitors of happiness.

I want to build a ladder
from my heart to my head
so the angels can move freely.

Seeing Emily Dickinson
in San Francisco

Outside City Lights
she greets me with a poem
that just came to her fully formed.

In the Union Street Bar
her friend begs her
to write it down, but she doesn't.

Instead, she takes me to the Union Hotel,
to her room where cockroaches
scatter in the sink.

Come on boy, she says, suddenly
naked. *Take your pencil and write
a beautiful poem inside of me.*

I do — it is — we fly around
in her toy sky looking for all
her lost poems.

In the morning, I buy her a cheese
omelette. She kisses me, sends me
back to the beckoning brightness.

My Best Poem

Last night I dreamed my best poem ever.
To save time, I wrote it all down
in elegant script on equal halves
of the night sky under my eyelids.

Whenever I closed one eye
to see what I was doing, the poem disappeared.
When I closed both eyes, the poem
reappeared only after the light
had dimmed way down.

By then I had composed
a new best poem to replace
the one that was all about last night,
because there was already
so much to write about today.

On a Mountainside

Our lunches are spread out
and there — a metallic green
sparkplug of a creature —
the elusive tiger beetle I've seen
only once before, when my boy
was young in another field.
On this mountainside —
with my soon-to-be wife,
stepdaughter, stepson,
and the family dog —
memory descends to christen
a new beginning.
I'm plunging again
into fathering territory,
the homing instinct as we
gaze on this unheralded
gift from the sky whose strangeness
adorns our intimacy,
freshens our aspirations,
compounds the pleasure
of this life we're in.

Newly Wed, Again

I thought the salt would never
leech from my wounds
or else I'd have to dream

my way back through creation
to those first feelings
of falling. So here we are

blooming like children's drawings
on the fridge, our twin hearts
revealing private history

and its requisite pain.
We make space for ourselves
the way branches make space

for sky, dousing for all
the water we can find
and we drink it in.

We drink it in.

About the Author

Richard Waring's poems have appeared in the *Comstock Review*, *Chest, Sanctuary, Contact II, Dark Horse*, the *American Journal of Nursing, Mothering, Inward Springs*, the *Journal of the American Medical Association*, and other publications. He has been anthologized in *The Pocket Poetry Parenting Guide, Rough Places Plain: Poems of the Mountains*, and *Unitarian Universalist Poets: A Contemporary American Survey*, and has appeared on *Phone-A-Poem* and the cable TV show *BookBeat*. Richard has a B.A. in English Literature from Drew University and attended the Jack Kerouac School of Disembodied Poetics at Naropa Institute, where he studied the poetry of William Carlos Williams with Allen Ginsberg. From 1982 to 1988, he edited *Zonë, A Feminist Journal for Women and Men*. In 1992, he was the writing workshop leader at the Star Island Conference on the Arts. His chapbook, *Listening to Stones*, was published in 1999 by Pudding House Publications. He hosts the Workshop for Publishing Poets reading series at Newtonville Books in Newton, Massachusetts. A long-time resident of Belmont, Massachusetts, where he raised a son and daughter, Richard now lives in neighboring Arlington with his wife and her children. He is a senior layout artist for the *New England Journal of Medicine*.

A Word about the Type

This book was set in Baskerville, a type designed by 18th century
English entrepreneur John Baskerville (1706–1775).
Born in rural Worcestershire, he moved to the city
of Birmingham as a boy, and became a writing teacher
and stonecutter. Soon, however, he began manufacturing
"japanned" ware, highly varnished, hand-painted pieces of
bric-a-brac, and by the time he was forty, he was rich.
But his first love was "the beauty of letters," and
eventually he established his own press. Baskerville
not only designed typefaces — he also cast and set
the type, made improvements in paper and in the printing
press, and designed and published books and newspapers.
The Baskerville face is known as a transitional face,
as it bridges the gap between Old Style and modern type design.
As typefaces developed through the ages, the contrast
between the thick and thin strokes, originally based on
the movements of a wide-nibbed pen or brush, gradually increased.
Baskerville's letters are light and elegant, with a fairly strong
thick-thin contrast and such graceful design features
as the unusual curve of the tail on the Q.
Baskerville produced type of such extraordinarily
high quality that jealous critics used to claim the sharpness
and clarity of his letterforms gave them "headaches."